Buying Your First Boat

Rules of the Road
for
Power Boaters and Sailors

F. C. Pierce

RULES OF THE ROAD
for power boaters and sailors

Buying Your First Boat

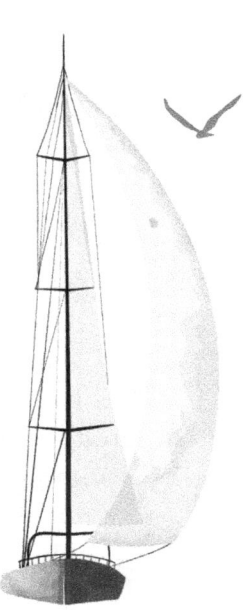

F.C. Pierce

Published by

Ocean Rose
(imprint of Random Bits)

Other publications can be found at
www.fcPIERCE.com

Copyright © 2017 by Craig Pierce
All Rights Reserved
This book or any portion thereof may not be
reproduced or used in any manner whatsoever
without the express written permission
of the copyright owner except for the use
of brief quotations in a book review.

Cover and Text Design by StickyEarth.com

Library of Congress Control Number:
2017959128

First Paperback Edition
ISBN 978-0-9762764-0-1

Dedication

*To Clarence,
faithful Springer Spaniel of my youth,
always ready to go for a sail.*

Acknowledgements

It is practically a cliché to acknowledge that an author needs help putting a book together. It is patently obvious to anyone who has ever tried. The (relatively) easy part for me was getting the rules down on paper. Making them informative, grammatically correct and (hopefully) entertaining required a "team effort." Left to my own devices, this book would still be languishing on my computer in the "To Do" file.

First and foremost, I have to thank Alexa Pierce, my life partner, major cheerleader and original editor who supported the idea, reminded me that I needed to write it, ("You don't want any incompletions in your life. Do you?"), and kept gently (sometimes not so gently) asking me: "Is it done yet?" Thank you, I love you!

I also want to thank Terri Breier who took over the editing of the book when it became clear that asking Alexa to do "just one more little thing," was only going to disrupt what remained of our domestic bliss and tranquility. A "fresh pair of eyes" was just what the doctor ordered. Thank you!

Finally, this book would still be fermenting in the Internet distillery if not for the herculean efforts of Annette Murray, my publishing Doula, who gently but firmly cracked the whip over my head about deadlines and schedules that needed to be kept. She also had the patience to put up with my constant tinkering with the text to get it "just right." If not for her, I'd have tinkered myself into the next decade. Thank you! Your calm demeanor and positive feedback kept me from going down the rabbit hole — at least most of the time. As I've told you on several occasions, there's a special place in Heaven for people like you willing to help writers publish their work.

Table of Contents

Preface 1

New or brokerage? 7

Rule 1: *Does the mere thought . . . make your heart beat faster?* 13

Rule 2: *Search globally, buy locally* 17

Rule 3: *You don't know what you don't know* 21

Rule 4: *Everything on a boat is a compromise* 25

Rule 5: *Buy the biggest boat you can afford to maintain* 31

Rule 6: *Every boat problem has a solution* 35

Rule 7: *A good deal doesn't make it a good boat* 41

Rule 8: *A good boat is a good deal* 45

Rule 9: *Trust but verify* 53

Rule 10: *Every buyer becomes a seller* 69

Appendix 71

Glossary 74

About the author 83

Preface

If you're reading this page, you are probably considering the purchase of your first boat. Not a rowboat, or a canoe, or a dinghy, but a vessel large enough to take you, your family and friends out on the ocean or some other body of water, and you are uncertain about the process. Is it like buying a car? How big a boat do you need? Must you have a license to drive a boat?* Where should you start your search? In short, what are the *Rules of the Road* for buying a boat?

You're not alone. During my years as a yacht broker, I heard these questions and many others from first time boat buyers. They are the same questions I asked myself when I went looking for my first sailboat in the late 60's. Back then I was a twenty-one-year-old kid with a little money in my pocket and a desire to get out on the water. There was no Internet, no *Yacht World*, only pictures in magazines and newspapers, descriptions from owners and brokers over the telephone, and prowling through boatyards on my own. I put a lot of miles on my Volvo P-1800 going from boat yard to boat yard in New England.

---

*The simple answer is "no." However, if you intend to hire out your boat and yourself then the answer is "yes." You will need a Captain's license from the Coast Guard. See General Reference in the Appendix.

I saw lots of boats and, probably like you, kept looking for the perfect one. When people asked me what kind of boat I was looking for, I really couldn't tell them except in general terms: "A sailboat I could take cruising." I didn't really know what that meant. What kind of cruising? Local? Coastal? World Wide? It was too vague.

I ended up with a 36-foot wooden Yawl that had started life in the Great Lakes. The present owner had shipped the boat to his home in Westport, Massachusetts, where he sailed her for several years before putting the boat on the market. I saw her in early April, still under winter cover, and bought the boat the following week — no sea trial, no survey, no broker. I'd fallen in love with the boat. What I'd forgotten — if I even knew it at the time — was the old saying, "Love is blind."

I stepped onboard for the first time in Mid-May when I sailed or, more precisely, tried to sail her down to my home port of Guilford, Connecticut, on the northern shore of Long Island Sound. I got as far as New London, Connecticut, before the engine — a Gray Marine 30 HP gas engine — overheated and I had to turn it off. I tried calling the Coast Guard but got no response (I was to find out later, that no one had connected the radio antenna to the radio when the boatyard "Spring Commissioned" the boat). The tide was against me and the wind was in my face. It took four hours to go five miles, and I would probably still be trying if a passing fishing boat hadn't graciously towed me to the town dock — an ignominious arrival in my first port.

It took two days to find a mechanic willing to look at the engine — it was the height of the spring launching season — and another two to replace the worn-out hose with the tiny pinprick holes that had allowed the coolant, under pressure, to escape the supposedly "closed" system. I also looked, without success, for an electrician to "fix" the VHF radio. The mechanic took pity on me, checked the radio, then "as a matter of habit" he informed me afterward, checked the connections where he found the disconnected antenna wire at the base of the mast, and connected it (AND WRAPPED THE CONNECTION IN WATER PROOF TAPE). In typical New England fashion, all he said after he pointed out the problem was "First boat?" I nodded. He smiled.

It was a sober and embarrassing start to what would become one of the happiest times in my young life. And it could have been avoided, which is exactly why I have written this book — the book I wish I'd had back in 1968.

Why Should You Listen to Me?

In the years since, I've owned two more sailboats, both fiberglass, as well as a charming 16-foot wooden daysailer. I have cruised the East Coast from Nova Scotia through the Chesapeake, from Florida through the Bahamas; from San Diego to the San Francisco Bay in California, including the Channel Islands as well as Catalina; lived on board a 30' sailboat for several years, and worked as a yacht broker in Santa Barbara for 10 years. I've learned a thing or two about what does and doesn't work when it comes to boats.

I developed my "Rules" over the decade I spent buying and selling boats with my clients. Being a licensed, professional yacht broker requires not only a deep knowledge of boats, but the ability to listen to the clients' needs and respond positively with information that supports their goals. I learned to ask questions, not only about the kind of boat they wanted to own but their plans for how they intended to use the boat and with whom. The answers, along with my own acquired knowledge, formed the basis for this book.

Because I have been on both sides of the boat sales process, I know what it takes to make it successful. As you read through the chapters, you will see that I have "charted a course" to find the right boat for you. While I encourage you to follow my directions, as with most endeavors, there is more than one way to get where you want to go. You are the Captain! I am merely the navigator.

I make only one request. When you get your first boat, please send me a picture at: fcpiercewriter@gmail.com. I never tire of pictures of boats and their new owners.

All the forms that appear in this book are available as 8.5x11 PDFs that you can print out. Just email me a request for them at fcpiercewriter@gmail.com and I will email them to you.

Happy Hunting!

BUYING YOUR FIRST BOAT

New or Brokerage*?

Like a new car there's something exciting, even exhilarating, about a new boat. Both are shiny and have that new vehicle smell. Both come with pristine warranties and manuals. Untouched. You are the first owner.

However, most drivers don't begin with a brand-new car. Why should you start with a brand-new boat? Let's see if it makes (dollars and) "cents" for you.

Consider the Cost

Let me use the following example. Say you want to buy a new 36' sailboat, and the dealer says it will cost around $180,000 (the BASE PRICE). Then you decide to add the following equipment: radar, electronics, extra sails, cockpit cushions (ouch!), a self-furling system, and upgraded anchor equipment. Now, the price tag rises to over $220,000, plus sales tax. Five years later, that same boat — including all the equipment you have added — will list for $140,000–$150,000. Depending on demand, it may sell for as low as $132,000.

*"Brokerage" refers to previously owned boats, sail or power, offered for purchase through a Yacht Brokerage. Brokers do not refer to them as "used."

Perhaps you're thinking, "OK, I'll just buy a smaller boat." A new 25' sailboat costs between $70,000 and $120,000. It will depreciate by the same or greater value percentage-wise over the next five years. A new 36' powerboat starts at over $225,000 and goes up from there.

Based on this information, why would anyone buy a new boat?

Why New?
There are reasons people consider buying a new boat. If…

- They have already owned several boats;
- They plan to keep their boat for more than 10 years;
- Over time, they have found a model that has fulfilled their needs;

Then purchasing a new boat makes good sense.

Of course, without new boat owners there would be NO boat owners. If a new boat makes sense to you, then by all means buy one with my blessing.

Why Brokerage?
If, however, this is your first boat I would urge you to start with a brokerage vessel. Despite initial appearances, a new boat is NOT the same as a new car. Unless you plan to use

her every day for work or move aboard, a boat is a luxury, recreational item (like an RV).

The good news is that there are many excellent, pre-owned boats available. Boats five years old or less may already have everything you want installed. Seaworthy vessels over six years old are also available.

A note here about terminology: *Yacht dealerships sell new boats. Yacht Brokerages sell used boats. Dealerships have Brokerage divisions, just as car dealerships have a used car division. Three states, Florida, Virginia and California require yacht brokers and salespeople to be licensed. In all of the others, there are associations but no licensing requirements.*

I recommend that you make a list of what you want in a boat *before* you start looking at the brochures and online pictures. You may not even know yet if you want a powerboat or a sailboat. In later chapters, we will discuss how to winnow down your choices. But first, a cautionary warning:

Buy in Haste, Regret at Your Leisure

I know it can be tempting. You go to a boat show and see the "boat-of-your-dreams." The salesman tells you that there's a "special boat show price" that includes everything you see on board. The booth right next door has a "special boat show financing rate" for which you qualify. All you need to do is plunk down 20% and they'll even roll the sales tax into the monthly payment. **Wow!!!** That twenty percent matches the dollar amount you planned to pay for a brokerage boat. Now you can get a brand-new one that's much bigger and much better for the same amount of money (and of course a monthly fee)!

"WOW!!!" is right! "Watch-Out-Wally" (or Wendy) and stop right there! Take a deep breath. Remember this acronym. B-O-A-T stands for "Bring-Out-Another-Thousand." The only leisure-time activities that may be more expensive per use are polo and private aviation. The best thing you can do for yourself and for those who love you is to STOP, walk away and seek help — like this book.

Time Is Your Friend

Give yourself some "breathing room." If you're new to boating, first join a sail or a powerboat club. Make friends with fellow boaters and go out on their boats (offer to "crew" for free). There are classes offered by the Power Squadron* for boaters (sail and power). Sign up for these. Once you have taken some or all these actions, then you are ready to start looking for a boat of your own.

Don't Feel Discouraged

The road to your first boat is not as long or as arduous as you think. Follow the Rules I suggest in this book and you'll find so many good boats that the hardest (and the most fun) part will be choosing which one is best for you. The right boat is out there waiting for you. Let's go find it!

*See Appendix, General Reference

BUYING YOUR FIRST BOAT

RULE NO 1

If the mere thought of your boat doesn't make your heart beat just a little bit faster, then you have the wrong boat.

Never break Rule #1! When it comes to boats, you need more than love. But without it, no boat, no matter how shiny and bright with all of the latest gadgets, will be the *right* boat for you. I know that can seem straightforward enough, but it can get lost in all the paperwork and due diligence that goes into buying your boat — especially if this is your first boat. The following chapters discuss the reality checks you should take. But if you don't follow Rule #1, adhering to the other nine won't get you what you want.

The "Defining Spec"

With that in mind, let's take the first step on your road to purchasing the boat of your dreams.

You may have already decided what kind of boat you're looking for, a powerboat or a sailboat. You may have even narrowed down your search to the size you want. But first, I want you to take a moment and write down what you want the boat for. This is not a random exercise, it's what I call the defining specification(s) or **"*Defining Spec*"** for your boat search.

Be as specific as you can. A good start is: "I want a 30-foot powerboat that I can take offshore to go fishing with my friends." Or "I want a 26-foot sailboat with a cockpit and shelter large enough to take my wife and two kids for day sails in the bay." But you'll want to add more specifics. Take some time to write these down, while keeping the following questions in mind:

- Where will you be using the boat?
- What kind of experience do you have on the water?
- How much time, if any, have you spent on a boat similar to the one you're considering?
- How often will you use the boat?
- How long is the boating season where you intend to use it?
- How much help will you need to use the boat?
- How enthusiastic is your spouse/partner about getting a boat?

I'm sure you have other questions and considerations as well. The point is the more specific you are about how you will use the boat, the closer you will be to finding the right boat for you.

The Defining Spec will also clarify some of the smaller, yet important, details. If you're looking for a 30-foot powerboat for offshore fishing, you will want twin engines for safety reasons, as well as speed. Likewise, a 26' daysailer and

26' cruising sailboat serve different purposes. A daysailer generally uses an outboard motor, while the cruiser would require a small inboard diesel engine. This distinction can be important when considering maintenance costs.

You should carry the Defining Spec with you on paper as you search online and in person.* Not only will it save you time and, ultimately, money, but will ensure that the vessel you purchase is indeed the heart-racing boat of your dreams!

---

*I've left room in the back of this book for notes where you can write down the Defining Spec — as well other notes — about the boats you see. You can also email me at fcpiercewriter@gmail.com to request a letter-sized PDF of a blank Defining Spec similar to what follows on the next page.

RULE №1 ~ Defining Spec

I want a _____

that can_____

_____

Where will you be using the boat? _____

_____

What kind of experience do you have on the water? _____

_____

How much time, if any, have you spent on a boat similar to

the one you're considering? _____

How often will you use the boat? _____

How long is the boating season where you intend to use it? ___

How much help will you need to use the boat? _____

How enthusiastic is your spouse/partner about getting a boat?

_____

Additional Information

_____

_____

_____

Email fcpiercewriter@gmail.com for an 8.5 x 11 PDF of this form that you can print out.

RULE №2

Search globally, buy locally.

At first glance, this rule seems contradictory. Why should I search globally, if all I'm going to do is buy locally? I've conflated two seemingly disparate ideas in order to make them easier for you to remember.

By example, let me tell you a story. Perhaps it will sound familiar.

Once upon a time, Bruce Boatbuyer goes online looking for a boat to buy. He finds one he likes, contacts the listing broker, and asks a bunch of questions. He likes the broker's answers and makes an appointment to see the boat the following weekend. He makes the two-hour drive only to discover that it's not what he expected at all. Did he ask the wrong questions or did the Broker mislead him (he did mention that she needed a "little work")? Either way, Bruce is disappointed. Since he's already made the trip, he decides to look around for any other boats that might interest him. He sees a few but nothing catches his eye.

"Oh well" Bruce sighs, as he climbs back into his car for the long drive home. "I guess it's back to the Internet." All he has to show for his time is several print outs of boat "specs" and several out-of-town broker's cards in his pocket.

The end.

Who Is Representing You?

What is wrong with this scenario? Ask yourself, "Who represents "*Bruce*" in those interactions?" The answer is "no one." Those brokers have a fiduciary responsibility to the seller, *not Bruce (or you)*. That does not mean they have done anything underhanded or unethical; it simply means that they *must* represent the seller's interests above all others.

What do you do? This is where Rule #2 — *Search Globally, Buy Locally* — fits.

Here is the scenario I recommend *before* you go looking for boats.

Step 1: Go to the harbor
where you *plan to keep your boat*.

Step 2: Interview the local brokers
in the area to get a feel for them and their offices. Ask each broker questions to determine if he is:

- Familiar with the kind of boat you're looking for
- Interested in helping you search for that boat
- Understands and agrees with your Defining Spec
- Knowledgeable

Step 3: Repeat this process
until you find a broker you like and retain him or her* as your representative. Remember that

---

*A note here about gender usage. There are many good brokers who happen to be female. I have worked with several, and while the perception is (still) that boating is a man's world, I have had female clients who were knowledgeable and very competent boaters. I've tried to balance the use of 'he' with 'her' in this booklet. For the reader, please do not assume any gender bias, either in this book or in your choice of a Broker.

the buyer never pays the broker a fee — the broker receives her commission from the seller's proceeds!

Step 4: Allow your broker to be your advocate and handle the initial legwork, which she can do much better than you — after all, that is her job. In this role, she will:

- Search for boats with and for you.
- Talk to the listing broker about each boat that interests you before you view it.
    a) Your broker knows the right questions to ask
    b) There is a good chance she may know the seller's broker
    c) Perhaps she even knows the boat firsthand from showing it to other clients
- Your broker may have a "pocket" listing (see Glossary of Terms), on the right boat for you.

Step 5: Gather all the necessary information from your broker *before* you view the boats for sale. That way you can remain objective, make informed decisions, and be sure the boat which makes your heart beat faster (see Rule #1) also meets all of your criteria.

Step 6: Put the broker's knowledge and experience to work for you. Whenever possible, take him with you to view the boats you have discussed.

Note: *If the broker you've chosen does not fit my description, I suggest that you find another broker Usually that won't be necessary. Do your* *homework, interview each candidate thoroughly, and you will find the most helpful broker for you.*

One Possible Exception to Rule #2 *Search Globally, Buy Locally*

Nowadays, the Internet allows you to look anywhere in the world. Perhaps you're looking for a sailing adventure to bring your first boat to your home harbor from an overseas location. Maybe your Defining Spec specifies that you want to be in a particular foreign country or go on an extended cruise. In these situations, *use a broker in that country*. He should have the inside knowledge you'll depend upon to outfit your boat for the trip. Otherwise, I recommend following Rule #2.

BROKER _____

MARINA _____

CELL PHONE _____

BROKER _____

MARINA _____

CELL PHONE _____

RULE №3

You don't know what you don't know.

The reality is that no one, including the best yacht broker in the world, can possibly know everything about every boat on the market. If you ask ten boaters about a certain vessel, you're likely to get ten different answers. It all depends on what each person is looking for in a boat. If you are new to boating, it can seem like asking several blind men to describe an elephant. But don't lose sight of your Defining Spec. What are you looking for in a boat? *That's* the question. Read everything you can about a particular boat model, including reviews, magazine articles and blogs. Ask owners either in person or online through owner groups. But your best ally will be your broker. That's why picking him is important.

Fortunately, there are several things you can still do to help with the decision.

Match the Broker to the Defining Spec

As a first-time buyer, you'll want to find a broker who is familiar with the type of boat you're interested in. I'm not talking about generalities here. If the Defining Spec is taking your family on weekend cruises, then make sure you select a broker who has done that. Likewise, if you plan on day sailing or in-harbor entertaining, find a broker who has that same experience. In each case, the broker will directly apply her hands-on experience in the search process. She can tell you why she chose the boat she did and help you narrow down your choices. Without such firsthand guidance, it's easy to get side-tracked.

If you have bought a home, then you'll likely recall how overwhelming and confusing that process can be. You can get caught up in the thrill of it all and lose track of what you were looking for in the first place. You need a good real estate agent to guide you through the process and keep you safe. Likewise, you want a yacht broker who can do the same.

Owner's Groups

Once you have narrowed down your choices to a few different boats, a good source of additional information is Owner's Groups. The Internet has made these groups accessible to the general public. Usually, there is a "public" page, and the owners are happy to answer most questions. They may also allow you to join or post a conversation thread, which can provide even more insight into the boat. Typically, these websites include a page that lists members' boats for sale, as well. To find these groups, do a Google search for the model that interests you. Example: Catalina (sail), Sea Ray (power).

Magazine Research

Another good resource is boating magazines. For sailboats, these include: *Sail*, *Wooden Boat*, *Sailing*, and *Good Old Boat*. The latter two publish reviews of both new and older models every month, with "pros and cons" and market value. Two excellent powerboat publications are *Motor Boating* and *Yachting* magazine, which have reviews of new power boats in every issue.

I also recommend *Practical Sailor* and *Practical Boater*, which are the maritime versions of *Consumer Reports*. While they don't have individual boat reviews, they do run tests on boating equipment, which you will find enlightening and valuable. Because they do not accept advertising, they are unbiased...however, this makes them more expensive. You can generally find these publications alongside most of the other boating magazines at newsstands or bookstores, and possibly at your local library.

Additionally, there are local boating newspapers that publish weekly or monthly. Besides covering local boating events, issues, and concerns, there is always a "For Sale" section. Check your local newsstand or library.

BUYING YOUR FIRST BOAT

RULE NO 4

Everything on a boat is a compromise.

As your search progresses, you will discover one of the "facts of life" for boaters: *your dreams always envision a larger boat than your pocketbook can afford* which leads directly to Rule #4 summarized as follows: *Be prepared to compromise.*

Boat designers and builders are well aware of this rule. They spend lots of time and money researching what their buyers want, and they try to provide those features, while maintaining price as an important consideration. First-time buyers can find it daunting to differentiate between what is necessary and what is "nice to have."

That's why I urge you to develop and write down the Defining Spec *before* you start your search. *I can't stress this idea strongly enough.* Keep it with you *on paper*. And remember, the only *perfect* boat is the one in your dreams.

Creating Your Wish List

If you are at the point where you have seen several boats which all fit the Defining Spec, now is the time to fine tune your search, by writing down your "wish list."

BUYING YOUR FIRST BOAT

I'm sure you can appreciate the importance of clarifying what you want vs what you need. Your wish list will help you define this. Divide your list into two columns "Must Have" and "Would Like" as in the example below.

Wish List: 30' Sailboat

Must Have(s)	Would Like(s)
Roller Furling Head Sail	Furling Mainsail
Wheel Steering	Auto Pilot
6'2" Headroom	Aft Cabin
Refrigeration	Diesel Stove
Radar	Chart Plotter
Companionway Dodger	Cockpit Tent
120% Headsail	Spinnaker
Marine Radio	Electric Anchor Windlass

Wish List: 30' Power Boat

Must Have(s)	Would Like(s)
Diesel Engine	Twin Diesel Engines
Power Anchor Windlass	Bow/Stern Thrusters
Radar/Fish Finder	Tuna Tower
2 Bait Tanks	Cold Fish Storage Tank
6'4" Headroom	Two Full 6' Berths
Working Galley	Room For A TV/ Entertainment Center
Stand Up Room In The "Head"	Composting Toilet
Diesel Generator	AIS*

*Automatic Identification System

The lists to the left are for demonstration purposes. Naturally, yours should have items that are of particular interest to you and the people who use the vessel with you. Items such as a shore power cord and an FM radio/CD player (or whatever the latest piece of entertainment equipment you want to use) may fall on either side of your list. Items such as life preservers, spare anchors, dock lines, and safety lines are safety items and should be considered "Must Haves."

What you put on the list is up to you. Don't let cost deter you. If they are "Must Haves" then perhaps only look at boats that already have them.

One important note here: *Electronics decrease in value more rapidly than the boat itself. If you want radar on your boat but new radar is too expensive, don't knock it off your list. Many boats have radar that works well even if it is seven or eight years old. If you want to have radar that integrates with a chart plotter, it may need an upgrade. Check with a marine electronics installer.*

If you're not sure on which side to place the item(s), ask your broker's opinion. Again, she should be able to tell you how important each of the items are to her in her boating experience.

Compare the inventory on a boat you're interested in to your lists. How closely do they match up? It's an important question to ask yourself because it goes into the next section we're going to discuss.

Price Becomes a Consideration

Working from your list, the time will come when you will need to make some financial decisions. Chances are that somewhere in the back (or front) of your mind, you have already determined a fixed dollar amount (as well as an overall "size" of the vessel) you are willing to spend on your boat. Now is the time to revisit that decision.

Here are two key questions to ask:

1) How long do I plan to keep this boat?
2) How often will I be able to use it?

If your answer to the first question is longer than seven years, then you are making a long-term investment. If it's less, you should consider a "starter boat." That is a boat with the basic necessities, perhaps smaller, certainly less expensive than you had planned on spending, because you'll want to save that money for your next boat. (When I was a California broker, a boat changed hands every five years on average.) Likewise, I would make the same suggestion if the answer to Question #2 is "occasionally." In each case, you are "trying on" a lifestyle choice, like golf or skiing. Give yourself the time and the opportunity to see if it turns out to be a "good fit."

Time availability is also a factor. If you are single, you may have plenty of extra time. If you are married with a family, you may not be able to get out on the water as often as you would hope. Perhaps for now, you should consider a smaller boat that you can trailer and keep in your backyard. This is your *first* boat. It doesn't have to be your only boat or your last one.

If the Defining Spec includes your entire family, make sure you include them in the decision about which boat to purchase. The next rule should help you with that.

Wish List

Must Have(s)	Would Like(s)

Blank wish list available as 8.5 x 11 PDF. Email fcpiercewriter@gmail.com

RULE №5

Buy the biggest boat you can afford to maintain.

Buying your first boat is often compared to trying to take a picture of an iceberg. No matter how close you get to it, 90% is still beneath the surface, out of sight. Likewise, total boat maintenance cost is only "visible" *after* you've owned the boat for a while. Here are additional "Rules of the Road" that can help reduce the "surprises" of boat maintenance.

- Avoid wood trim and all wooden boats (for now).
- Find out the annual insurance cost up-front—ask the present owner if you have a specific boat in mind.
- Research the annual mooring costs in the harbor where you plan to keep your boat.
- If you are in a location where your boat needs to be hauled out every winter, check with local yards and get their rates.
- Stay away from a "fixer-upper" boat. You'll spend all of your time doing just that.

When you submit an offer for a particular boat, make sure that you have a survey done—this is similar to a home inspection for a house sale. It will provide a more complete picture of the boat's present condition, and list immediate maintenance requirements, called "Deferred Maintenance."

There will be another list called "Regular Maintenance," which states ongoing repair needs. (More about this in Rule #9 — *Trust But Verify*.)

Boat storage is usually defined (and charged) by the overall length of the boat known as the LOA. Boat maintenance also depends on the vessel's size. A larger boat means larger engines, taller masts, bigger equipment, etc.

Once you have all this information, the Defining Spec may change. Be grateful that you did it *before* purchasing a boat you can't afford to keep. That does not mean you can't get a boat, it means "adjusting the picture" to fit your present situation.

As I've said before, buying a boat is making a lifestyle choice. Personally, I think it's a great choice! A boat provides recreation. It can bring families together. It gets you out in nature and teaches life skills. But it also makes demands on your time and your discretionary income.

If you meet resistance from your spouse/partner, or you have other concerns, I encourage you not to give up on your dream. Consider renting a boat for day outings or chartering a boat for a week. See if the resistance abates. No matter the outcome, you will be in a better position to know how you want to proceed.

Financing Your Boat

Most first-time boat buyers don't finance the boat (unless it's a new boat). In general, I don't recommend borrowing to buy your first boat. Even if the bank or credit union is willing to lend the money, I wouldn't consider doing it unless you can pay off the entire amount in two or three years.

If you do choose to proceed with a loan, make sure to get pre-qualified for your intended price range by a lending company — your current bank, a financial institution you've dealt with in the past, or a credit union. There are companies that specialize in boat loans, which you can find online. Your broker should be able to provide a list of these institutions.

Be aware that financing your boat may limit your options. Your lender will send a list of requirements upon which financing decisions are based. For instance, they may not finance boats older than 10 years, a common practice when I was a broker. They may not finance new or "Brokerage" wooden boats. When I was working, the normal down payment was 20 percent, and most banks didn't extend financing beyond 10 years. In addition, interest rates fluctuate.

The bottom line: maintenance and financing are key factors that can influence how much boat you are able to afford, be sure to include them in your calculations.

RULE №5 ~ **Maintenance and Finance**

Maintenance

Annual Insurance Cost _____

_____

Annual Mooring Cost _____

_____

Haul Out and Storage Rates _____

_____

Deferred Maintenance _____

_____

Regular Maintenance _____

_____

Finance considerations

Boat age limit _____

Wooden boats permitted? _____

Down payment _____

Loan years _____

Interest rate _____

Email fcpiercewriter@gmail.com for an 8.5 x 11 PDF of this form that you can print out

RULE №6

Every boat problem has a solution.

By now, you've created your list of what is important and determined the price range for your purchase. After sharing this with your broker, he finds candidates that meet your criteria. Now it is time to go see these boats!

The top seven things to bring when you look at a boat are:

1) The Defining Spec (always keep this with you!).
2) The boat listing from your broker — usually from *Yacht World* or an online post.
3) Your Wish List (on paper).
4) A list of questions (also on paper) that you want to ask about the boat.
5) A notebook and pen to write down your impressions of each boat.
6) A camera to take pictures of each boat.
7) Whenever possible, bring your broker with you.

If your broker cannot join you, at least arrange for the two of you to talk while you're looking at these boats. FaceTime or a similar video messaging smartphone app is very helpful if you want to show your broker something while you're on the boat.

If you are viewing more than one boat, be sure to identify each set of pictures, especially if you are looking at several of the same model. Recording boat names is a good way to do this. Take the time to write down your notes and identify your pictures BEFORE you leave the boat. That way, you can get answers to any additional questions on the spot. Above all, don't feel rushed! Take all the time you need.

Look for Potential Issues

While you're onboard, you may notice a problem or two. An example might be that the cockpit on a fishing boat is smaller in person than it appeared in the pictures. Or when you stand in the cockpit of a sailboat, the dodger blocks your view forward. There will almost always be some problems with any given boat (See Rule #4 – *Everything on a Boat is a Compromise*).

Allow me to make a slight adjustment to Rule #6: <u>ALMOST</u> *Every Boat Problem Has a Solution*. If there is a *design* issue on a boat, you'll either have to live with it or move on to another model. If you hit your head on the companionway hatch every time you go below deck, that's a *design* problem for you. When you're standing in the cockpit of a sailboat and have to duck whenever the boom passes from one side to the other, that's a *design* problem for you. If you can't squeeze into the "head," it's a real *design* problem for you.

But such concerns as a dodger blocking your view forward on a sailboat, or the handrail being too low or too high when you move forward or aft on a motorboat, are merely design *flaws* that can be fixed. Take pictures of such issues and make note of them.

Two More Important Lists
These issues lead to another list, "Problems." Once you've narrowed your choices to several boats, ask your broker or a boat repair professional what the approximate cost would be to repair the problems you find. Having this list on paper is extremely important, because as you see more boats, the individual problems will begin to blur in your mind. When determining your finalists, you will want to go back to your notes to generate a third list, "Cost to Repair or Replace."

The same goes for your wish list. If you find a boat that fulfills all of the "Must Have(s)" but falls short on the "Would Like(s)," get a cost estimate for purchasing and installing these items. There are several large stores such as West Marine and Defender Marine with online catalogs as well as store locations. Since many of the employees are boat owners themselves — I worked at a West Marine store while I was outfitting my boat — they can help you navigate the many different models and options.

If you don't have access to a store, talk face-to-face with a boat mechanic or electrician, preferably a local one in the harbor where you plan to keep your boat. Again, your broker should be able to point you in the right direction. Another good source is a marine surveyor — I'll have more to say about that later.

All these lists may seem like a lot of work, but in the end, I assure you they will save time and *money* as well as clarifying your boat choices. You may end up moving items from "Must Have" to "Would Like" or vice versa. You may add new items or remove some altogether, based on their cost versus importance (to you). Perhaps your lists will even influence you to change your Defining Spec. At the very least, they will help to keep each boat that you see clear in your mind and assist in whittling down your choices.

Follow Your Heart, But Don't Ignore Problems

Remember Rule #1? That boat you are looking at might very well be making your heart beat so fast that you're tempted to undervalue a serious problem. It is human nature to decide "That's no big deal" or "I can live with that." But don't forget that you'll be dealing with this problem EVERY TIME you're on board the boat. Take a deep breath and return to the Defining Spec. Look over your list of "Must Haves" again…you may need to tweak these lists slightly, based on what you've learned from viewing the boats in person. You still won't *know* a boat until you've sailed or motored her for a while. You'll get a chance to test the boat out during your *sea trial* as part of the purchasing process. But the problems that you've found won't disappear on their own.

Have Faith in the Process!

It may take longer than you hoped, but don't give up and settle, simply because a boat has *some* of the items you want or because you're impatient to get out on the water. Keep looking! You're learning more about boats and boat ownership every time you look at a boat. That's invaluable knowledge which will serve you well. You're probably much closer to finding the right boat than you realize. Don't give up!

RULE NO 6 ~ **Problems and Solutions**

BOAT _____

MARINA _____

MAJOR DESIGN PROBLEMS _____

_____

_____

_____

MINOR DESIGN FLAWS _____

_____

_____

_____

ITEMS MISSING FROM WISH LIST _____

_____

_____

_____

COST TO REPAIR, REPLACE or INSTALL _____

_____

_____

_____

Email fcpiercewriter@gmail.com for an 8.5 x 11 PDF of this form that you can print out.

RULE №7

A good deal doesn't make it a good boat.

It is a mistake to believe that every seller *must or even wants to* sell his boat. The truth about sellers is:

- Some will consider selling their boat.
- Some want to sell but aren't in a hurry.
- Some need to sell…and quickly.
- Some don't (really) want to sell but they are "pushed" to sell (usually by a spouse/partner).

Which kind of seller are you dealing with? Your broker can help you to understand the situation, but there are several clues that might give it away. For example:

- *Asking price:* Is it way out of line with other boats of the same model year? What has the owner done in the way of upgrades to justify the price?
- *Difficult to make an appointment:* That's a no-brainer. An owner who wants to sell his boat will work hard to make it available for showings.
- *Questions go unanswered:* If either the seller or the seller's broker isn't particularly forthcoming and helpful, they may be hiding something about the boat.

The above examples of an owner who isn't motivated to sell his boat are obvious, and there are those with lesser degrees of resistance. Still, you may find it difficult to get the information you want and have requested. My advice is to pass on those boats for the time being. There are plenty of good boats and sellers ready to help you.

The Desperate Seller

At the opposite end of the spectrum is the owner who is desperate to sell his or her boat. The price lists below market value and it appears that you are getting a lot more boat for your money, both in terms of size and features. It is doubly important to remember Rule #5 — *Buy the Biggest Boat You Can Afford to Maintain*. Go over this boat thoroughly with your list firmly in hand, and your broker on call. Desperate sellers typically have performed NO maintenance on the vessel in several seasons. You may be facing a significant amount of deferred maintenance.

A Strong Word of Caution

You should never:

- Give an owner any money until he produces a clear title and a bill of sale to you.
- Pay to have any work done on the boat until you have a signed sales agreement. And then only pay the service provider, not the seller.

- Be rushed into signing an agreement concerning the vessel—take all the time you need to make sure it is the best choice for you.
- Base a boat's value on how much money you can save by buying it "NOW." Remember, *"You Don't Know What You Don't Know."* is especially true here.

In general, it is wise to follow the old adage which has guided people for many years: "If it sounds too good to be true, it probably is." There are plenty of good boats with sellers who are ready to help you in any way they can. Deal with them first.

BUYING YOUR FIRST BOAT

RULE №8

A good boat is a good deal.

By this time, you are at the point where you have narrowed down your choices to several boats. You have applied Rule #1 — *Does the Mere Thought... Make Your Heart Beat Faster?* — as well as created the lists for each boat. The financing is in place. As the saying goes, you "have all your ducks in a row."

Good! Now it's time to make an offer!

Ready to Make Your Offer

Once again, your broker's knowledge and experience should steer you through this part of the process. There are two helpful online guides, BUCValu.com and NADAguides.com/boats (by the National Auto Dealers Association), that provide general price guidelines for pre-owned boats based on the model year and overall condition. I found the BUC Valu reports to be more in line with market values. In addition, your broker can look up "Sold Boats" on Yachtworld.com, which is especially helpful if the boat model hasn't changed significantly over the years and most of the "extras" like radar and electronics are already onboard. Keep in mind, there is some difference in pricing by region, which can also be valuable to you in your decision-making process.

One important caveat here...
If your broker is representing both you and the seller (because it's his listing), he or she is obligated to disclose this BEFORE an offer is made, to give you the option of choosing another broker to represent you financially in the sale. I mentioned earlier that the listing broker has a fiduciary responsibility to get the best price he can for his or her client. As you can see, this may lead to a conflict of interest between you (Buyer) and the broker. This isn't personal, it's business, you need to make the decision that feels most comfortable.

One workable solution I have used is to have another broker in the office — not involved with the deal — represent you in the negotiation.

Reminder:
THE BUYER NEVER PAYS THE BROKER A FEE.

Another option is to have a lawyer represent you during the negotiations. Of course, you will pay them directly, which can be expensive. If the sale is complicated, however, then it's a good idea to have an attorney's counsel.

Over the years, I dealt with each of these situations and experienced positive outcomes. It all depends on your comfort level.

Making Your Offer

If you have followed my *Rules of the Road* and:

- Looked online for comparable boats (make/model/year/equipment);
- Used your lists to compare boats;
- Researched the costs to do the upgrades or maintenance items you want;
- Discussed the offer with your broker or an impartial third party;

then ask your representative to initiate an *Offer to Purchase Agreement*.

Offer to Purchase Agreement

You have already narrowed the price range through the lists you have created from the boats that you have seen, the process should be simple, right? It is in theory, but when you see it in writing, you may have second thoughts. Too much? Too little? Is there a formula I can use? The simple answer is "no." Just like every boat, every seller is slightly different. But the seller who wants to sell his boat has done his homework and he has come up with a price that he feels is realistic (at least to him). This price may be based on the research he and his broker have done on sites such as BUCValu.com and *sold boats* on YachtWorld.com. A smart seller knows that you're looking there as well. Don't be surprised if his "asking" price is at or near the top $ range for his boat model. As an example, let's use the following scenario.

The combined average (BUC Val plus *sold boats* on YachtWorld) of a recent (5-6 yrs. old) 28' powerboat in good condition with twin gas engines is between $55-$65K. The seller has priced his boat at $65k. Your initial walk through hasn't turned up any major problems, but the upholstery is worn out and you'd like to replace it. You'd also like to upgrade the electronics. The hull needs a good waxing and may need to be repainted within the next several years. You run the numbers and find out that new upholstery will cost $1,200 (inside and out). New electronics is $3,500, and awl gripping (painting) the vessel is close to $6K. Still, you like the boat and you know that you can live with it just as it is for "a while."

What should your initial offer be? I'm going to suggest, $56K. If you're shaking your head, "I wouldn't offer him more than $50K max," you are looking at the wrong boat for you. Why? Because you're asking the seller to pay for changes that you'd like, or perhaps need, to do in the future versus what the boat needs as she sits in the water today. The seller has maintained his vessel; he probably knows that the upholstery will "eventually" need replacing or the boat will "eventually" need to be painted, but not today. That responsibility falls upon the new owner (see Rule #5 — *Buy the Biggest Boat You Can Afford to Maintain*).

You'll notice that I put the offer at just above the low end of the BUC Valu estimate. That serves two purposes. It doesn't offend the seller and it gives you more bargaining room. As I will discuss, you will have plenty of "outs" and opportunities to adjust the price based on the survey results (see Rule #9 — *Trust, But Verify*). But first you have to start the process somewhere and allow him to respond. It's a negotiation, and as in all negotiations, both sides will need to make compromises. Make the offer and see what happens. It's the only way you'll know for sure if this is the right boat for you.

Components of Your Offer

Your offer must be written, not verbal, and signed by you. It may or may not be done on a form, although most likely the broker's office will have a form for this purpose. This is a legal document. Read all of it thoroughly before you sign it. It should include:

- The name, model and year of the vessel.
- State registration, US Coast Guard document number, or both.
- The location of the boat.
- The name of the owner/seller.
- The name of the buyer (you).
- The price you are offering.
- The terms and conditions of the offer; e.g., subject to financing, survey and sea trial, plus any other contingencies that the buyer

includes in the offer. For sailboats, a "rigging survey" is often included on the list.
- A closing date—usually on or before 30 days from acceptance of the offer.
- The length of time the offer is in effect — which can be from 24 hours to seven days.
- An acknowledgement that the offer includes a check representing a 10% deposit, to be held by the buyer's brokerage firm in their escrow account. (Another VERY good reason to use a licensed broker.)
- Signature of the buyer (you), including the offer date.

Expect a Counteroffer

Once you make your initial *Offer to Purchase*, expect a counteroffer from the seller. He or she will probably lower the original *asking* price slightly, or change the terms of the purchase. You may have seen or heard the term, "As is, where is." This means, "I will sell you this boat for 'X' dollars with no contingencies, as she sits, with no warranties or other expectations."

I don't recommend this for first time buyers. See Rule #3 — *You Don't Know What You Don't Know* — that applies here in spades. Removing the contingencies leaves you with no "out" if you change your mind. Also, all insurance companies will require a professional survey before they will underwrite your vessel. You will be paying for this either way; if the surveyor finds any major issues, the insurance company will insist that you fix them before they insure it.

My suggestion is to respond to the seller's counteroffer with your *best and final* offer that includes your original contingencies.

This is a personal preference. I would allow the seller 48 hours to consider your best and final offer. You won't be pressing too hard, but you won't be providing a lot of time to mull it over, either. Based on my experience, if you've followed my suggestions, you will end up with a deal.

BUYING YOUR FIRST BOAT

RULE №9

Trust but verify.

Let's say you now have a signed *Purchase Agreement* from the Seller. The boat is almost yours! I know you're in a hurry to finish up, get on board, and start using your new-to-you boat. However, there are still a few hurdles to clear and they're important ones.

Before you sail off into the sunset, you will need to complete several surveys (similar to a home inspection), per the Terms and Conditions in your offer. This protects you by ensuring that the boat you purchase is "seaworthy" prior to signing the final sales agreement.

Clear the Contingencies

Whether you are purchasing a power boat or sailboat, you need to have the engine surveyed by a marine mechanic, and also hire a professional *(NAMS or SAMS - see Appendix)* marine surveyor to examine the entire vessel. This should include having the boat "hauled out for survey." The boatyard will quote a price for hauling out and keeping the boat in slings for about half an hour while the surveyor checks the bottom of the hull, unless it is already out of the water ("on the hard"). In that case, the hull survey should be done first, before launching the boat for the sea trial.

For a sailboat, order a rigging survey. The marine surveyor will check all the systems on the boat, including the rigging up to six feet above the deck. A sailboat rigging survey will inspect the rigging from the deck to the top of the mast. This is important! Without an examination of all the rigging, including the mast, you have no idea of its condition. If the mast is already down, make sure your surveyor checks the rig for fraying or splintering of the wire. You want these reports to give you as clear a picture as possible of the vessel's present condition.

Note: insurance companies consider the lifespan of the rig to be 10 years.

Sea Trial

This is usually the first contingency you want to check off. Unless the boat is "on the hard," it's easy to complete. The seller or the seller's broker, takes you out on the boat to see how it handles, and to give you the opportunity to test all the systems, confirming that they are in working order. These include: radar; bow and/or stern thrusters; the anchor gear, including windlass; winches; and halyards. You should test anything and everything that moves on the boat to find out if it is in working order. It may be the first time you've handled the boat on the water, making the sea trial more than a simple formality.

RULE 9

For Sailboats

If you are purchasing a sailboat, schedule the sea trial when there is the best chance of wind, usually afternoons. If there is little or no breeze, still raise the sails to see if you can get the boat to move. If not, don't accept the sea trial until you have the chance to experience the boat under sail. Why? Because you want to know how the boat handles in the wind.

Items to check:

- Does the tiller have a strong weather helm? Translation: When sailing close to the wind, do you have to fight the wheel/tiller to keep the boat from turning (heading up) into the wind? Sometimes you can lessen this by adjusting the sail trim. Try slacking the sails (letting them out) a little. If this doesn't help, there may be a design flaw. Ask the owner what he does about this problem and try his solution.

- Can you turn the wheel without too much resistance? Smaller boats often use wheels operated by pulleys. Check below the cockpit to see if something is inhibiting their movement. Perhaps the cables need adjusting (too tight or loose). Some steering systems are hydraulic and may need fluid. DON'T TRY TO FIX THE PROBLEM YOURSELF! This is important. It's not your boat yet. Allow the owner or the owner's broker to make those adjustments.

- Do the sails look baggy and frayed? Are they old and perhaps "blown out," i.e., stretched. If they don't hold their shape, you will be getting new sails as soon as you can afford them (brand new or slightly used).
- Do the sheets/lines look old and frayed when under load? Check them.
- If the head sail is self-furling, does it roll out without sticking? If not, have the surveyor check to see what is blocking it. It's possible that the furling drum needs to be greased or the furling line is frayed.
- Is it difficult to raise and lower the mainsail? Most sails use plastic lugs that fit into the mast slot, which can get stuck. Spraying with a silicone solution (such as Sail Dry) can help. NEVER use oil or oil-based sprays near your sails.

For All Boats

- Do the electronics work? Try each one and confirm that it is operational.
- Is there a noticeable vibration when the engine is under load? This may indicate that the engine shaft is out of alignment. Talk to your mechanic if he has not been on board for your sea trial. (The mechanic may feel this vibration at the dock.)

Mechanical Survey

Most sailboats have an auxiliary source of power, typically a small, 16-40 horsepower diesel engine. This engine should be capable of powering the sailboat at approximately five to seven knots (considered "hull speed") at 2500-2800 revolutions per minute (rpm). If the mechanic is unable to participate in the sea trial, he will run a "cold start" survey before you take the boat out. Mechanics can check out these engines at the dock, which includes running them "under load" using a "*dyno*" machine to accurately measure horsepower and torque.

For power boats, it is mandatory that the mechanic runs the boat on the water. A good mechanic will cold start the engine(s) and check the fluids for foreign materials by taking an oil sample. He will then run the engine(s) *under load* to see if there are any problems. It also gives the mechanic the opportunity to check the shifting mechanism. If it's hydraulic, he will check the fluid. If there is a generator, he should take an oil sample, then run it as well.

Note: *The mechanic will send his oil samples to a lab, which can take 3–5 business days to test.* **Wait for the results to come back** *before accepting the mechanical survey. Do not assume that, because the engine(s) ran smoothly, everything is fine. If the sample shows a high amount of metals, it could indicate a serious issue with the engine. The standard procedure in that case is:*

- *Replace the oil*
- *Run the engine under load for 10 hours (a full day at sea)*
- *Take new samples*

This delay may throw off the timing of the marine survey, but be patient and wait until you get the results back the second time, before doing the survey. This problem can be serious enough to warrant reconsidering the boat and perhaps canceling the offer. Discuss this with your broker and the mechanic before moving forward. If you have the slightest doubt about the engine(s), I would recommend that you cancel the sale and go back to your search list.

Marine (Vessel) Survey

The sole purpose of the marine, aka vessel, survey is to show the buyer the present condition and fair market value (FMV) of the boat. For insurance purposes, the surveyor must be SAMS/NAMS certified (See Appendix for website).

A survey can take a half-day to more than two days, depending on the size and condition of the vessel. Reputable surveyors charge a flat fee, based on vessel length. Your broker can give you a list of trusted surveyors they have worked with before. It's a good idea to ask boat owners in the harbor whom they would recommend as well. Compare the lists and if there is a name or two that is not on the broker's list, ask him why. Don't be afraid to "step on some toes" in the process.

A marine survey is part science, part the surveyor's experience. Surveyors are human, basing their recommendations on their previous experience. You want to choose one with a lot of experience to draw upon.

Although you may want to be aboard with the surveyor, give him or space to do his job. In fact, most surveyors don't want the buyer hanging over their shoulder as they go through the survey. I agree, it's not necessary. A good surveyor will go through the results with you, in person, aboard the vessel, once the inspection has been completed. He or she should point out any areas of concern and explain what that concern is. If it's unclear, ask questions right away, while you're looking at the problem. Take all the time you need to be sure you understand the surveyor's concerns, because they will become YOUR concerns if you buy the vessel.

The surveyor will present the findings in writing, which includes a list of the equipment found aboard, plus the present condition of the vessel. As a result of this survey, you will receive two lists: *Safety Issues* and *Maintenance Items*.

Equipment requiring immediate repair or replacement falls under the heading of *Safety Issues*. These will be considered by your lender and insurance company as well. You must correct all *Safety Issues* before the insurance company will issue a policy on the vessel. These are important and serious problems.

Common *Safety Issues* include, but are not limited to:

- Electrolysis - dangerously corroded items such as propellers/bronze fittings. Usually a result of faulty wiring or a lack of sacrificial zinc anodes connected to the vessel below the waterline.
- Inoperable pumps.
- Cracked or broken hoses, especially engine hoses.
- Leaky propane valves.
- Splinters in the rigging.
- Inoperable/expired carbon dioxide alarms.

Equipment or issues that should be addressed in the future, but don't affect the safety of the vessel, are considered *Maintenance Items*.

Common *Maintenance Items* may include:

- older rigging.
- inoperable electronics.
- baggy sails.
- undersized anchor or anchor chain.
- crazing in plastic ports or windows.

These items can seem subjective, but in the end, you decide how respond to the reported maintenance issues.

RULE 9

Fair Market Evaluation

At the end of the written report, your surveyor will include a ***Fair Market Value (FMV)*** evaluation of the vessel's worth as it sits AND what that value will be once the *Safety Issues* are corrected. Some surveyors also include ***Repaired Maintenance Issues*** in their FMV — make sure to ask which FMV they are providing!

The Survey Allowance

If you still want the vessel after the survey process, you and your broker will create what is called the ***Survey Allowance*** (unless you've signed an agreement to purchase the vessel "as is"). Be aware: this can be the most stress-filled document in the entire process. However, it is a very important document and another reason you want a broker that represents only you.

Your *Survey Allowance* will be based upon all the reports that you have received resulting from the sea trial, mechanical and hull surveys (plus rigging survey if it's a sailboat).

The letter may include items on the Maintenance list that are important to you, such as:

1) *Replace port(hole) windows due to "crazing."*
Crazing is caused by the exposure of plastic to ultraviolet light for extended periods. It first appears as small cracks, or *crazes,* within the window and over time will grow to obscure visibility. This happens to all plastic and is not a safety issue, but an aesthetic one. All power boats and motor sailors

use safety glass for the cockpit or steering station windows to avoid that problem.

2) *Replace a torn sail.*
   This is obvious and unless there are multiple tears or the sail is very old, the solution may be to have it patched instead.

3) *Upgrade mooring and anchoring gear.*
   Unless the lines are frayed and the chain is badly rusted, this is simply the surveyor's Maintenance Item and *not* a Safety Issue.

There may be numerous other suggestions — the surveyor works for you and provides the best information. You should seriously consider those suggestions before accepting the vessel.

How Much Weight Do You Give These Issues?

- *Safety Issues* MUST be fixed before completing the sale. You can't get the boat insured until they're fixed.
- *Maintenance Items* are fixed at the buyer's discretion. They don't cause a safety issue at the time of the sale and may never, but they are items that either make the vessel less esthetically pleasing or less efficient.

Caution: *If you have a long list of expensive maintenance items from the vessel and mechanical surveys, you are looking at a boat that might be categorized as a "fixer upper." I've previously stated that these are not good boats for first time buyers. I'd recommend that you cancel the sale and go back to your boat list.*

Creating the *Survey Allowance* Document
Option A

- State the issues as shown on the survey, using portions of the written survey as documentation.
- Document the projected cost, including written estimates from vendors, to fix the issues and repair or replace the items listed.
- Provide an estimated time frame to complete the repairs or replacements.
- Based on the above:
    1) The seller will pay for the repairs/replacements.
    2) The buyer will confirm the repairs/replacements are operational.
    3) The buyer will then pay the price stated in the final *Offer to Purchase Agreement.*

This would seem to be the fairest way to handle the issues, but remember that *only Safety Issues must be corrected.* I believe that the seller should pay for these. It may be thousands of dollars, but if he doesn't fix them, *they will appear on the next buyer's survey.* He knows this (or his broker should remind him) and is usually willing to have it done. However, paying for *all* of the *Safety Issues* will make the seller far less willing to pay for upgrades such as new port windows or sails. After all, only you benefit from these upgrades. Both sides need to be reasonable here.

Option B

- Show the seller the list of *Safety Issues* that need to be repaired.
- Show the documented cost to repair these items.
- Lower the *final* purchase price by that amount.
- Continue to the closing.

This process puts all of the cost of the maintenance items on you (the buyer), which may be fair, but you may still feel like you're overpaying.

Option C

- Require the seller to fix all of the *Safety Issues*.
- Lower the selling price by a dollar amount that will help to offset the *Maintenance Items* that you want to fix right away.

The normal process is to split the cost on the pressing items. It's up to you to decide which items those are. Updating electronics, especially if they are operational, will not happen. Purchasing a new sail will meet with the suggestion that you buy a used sail at a much lower price. That may be a good solution, but again the seller will not benefit and he probably won't help to pay for it. Of course, the seller has the right to propose a "counter-offer" to the *Survey Allowance* as well.

The Most Perilous Stage

You have arrived at the most perilous stage of the sales process. Both parties have expectations. The seller feels that the sale of his boat is close. You feel that the beginning of your "dream boat" adventure is within reach. Both parties would like this to go smoothly and move on. Most of the time it does. Most of the time the seller is reasonable, even offering to fix the *Safety Issues* that may come up *before* the survey reveals them. A smart seller may have already surveyed his boat when he put it on the market to avoid any surprises.

But in the heat of the moment, the seller may feel that you are trying to "squeeze" every nickel out of him. There's a limit to how much he's willing to spend to sell his boat.

"Maybe, I should just keep her," he thinks. "Fix her up and use her myself." At this moment, he's forgotten why he put the boat up for sale in the first place.

Conversely, you feel you're being pushed into buying a boat that is going to be nothing but a money drain.

"After all," you say to yourself or to your partner, "look at all the items that already need to be addressed. Maybe I should just walk away." You've forgotten what attracted you to this boat in the first place.

At this point a good broker will point out the following.

To the Seller:

- Why did he put the boat on the market in the first place? (Usually because he was not using it.)
- Maintenance, insurance and storage costs will continue if he doesn't sell the boat.
- *Safety Issues* have to be fixed, he must look at that as part of his cost to sell the vessel.

To You:

- Aside from the *Safety Issues,* what has to be done to make this boat serviceable?
    1) Maintenance items may be costly but are they necessary? In most cases there are alternatives that will work, at least temporarily, for you. Examples:
        a) Your cell phone has a GPS App.
        b) There are plenty of sail lofts that sell used sails in very good condition very inexpensively.
    2) Maintenance is an ongoing issue with a boat. You don't have to tackle every item at once.

- How long do you intend to own this boat? (Create an annual maintenance schedule that includes a few upgrades and fixes per season. See if this makes ownership easier for you).

- You've already invested money into this boat. Think carefully before you walk away as you'll be investing more money on another boat's survey process. In other words, you know a lot about this boat already.

In my experience, it all comes down to money and time. You will have to make the final decision.

A good broker will suggest a "cooling off" period of a day or two to give both parties a chance to reflect on what they want to do. And remember Rule #1 — *Does the Mere Thought...Make Your Heart Beat Faster?* — it's never more important than at this particular stage of the purchase.

A Happy Ending

Let's assume that these obstacles are overcome and you buy this boat, or the next boat you put through the process. Congratulations! There's still paperwork, closing statements, taking possession of the boat — I hope you have a great big party! — planning your first voyage as the new owner. There are plenty of things to keep you busy. I just want to give you one more "rule" to think about before you sail into the sunset.

RULE NO 9 ~ **Trust But Verify**

MARINE MECHANIC _____

PHONE _____

MARINE SURVEYOR _____

PHONE _____

RIGGING SURVEYOR _____

PHONE _____

SEA TRIAL NOTES

_____

_____

_____

_____

_____

_____

_____

Email fcpiercewriter@gmail.com for an 8.5 x 11 PDF of this form that you can print out.

RULE №10

Every buyer becomes a seller.

Why Now?
Here you are, a new boat owner. Why think about selling your boat now? Because you'll never be closer to "both sides of the coin" than you are at this moment. You won't know what you might have done differently about buying the boat until you've had some time and distance from the process, but you are very aware of what the seller did or didn't do. You see how much you counted on the expertise of your broker, the marine mechanic, the professional surveyor, and perhaps the rigger. Their information informed your decisions on the vessel that you now own.

What were they looking for and what did they find? You have a list of those items, many of them you may wish to fix right away. Some you will put off until later. In either case, they form the picture of your boat. Yes, *your* boat; How you maintain her is in your hands.

Buyer's Eyes
Recall all the things that you picked out in your mind that needed fixing, even before you got the reports. You looked at the boat with "Buyer's Eyes." Don't lose that perspective.

That's how the next potential owner will look at your boat when the time comes to sell her.

Start now. Take care of the items on the surveys. If not all at once, make a maintenance schedule and stick to it. Your boat will require ongoing maintenance, don't let that slip too far behind schedule. It's easier to do a little all the time instead of a lot all at once.

Enjoy Your Boat

But most of all, enjoy your boat! Take pride in her. Share her with your family and friends. Hopefully they will love her as much as you do. It's the beginning of a great adventure.

Please feel free to send me pictures of your boat and the adventures you take, even if it's only a day sail in the bay with your family. Those can be the best days of all.

Happy Boating!

Appendix

Reference Books

There are myriad books about the sea and sailing. Following is a list of several that I've used professionally and personally. I can recommend all of these books as being worth your investment of both time and money. They are listed alphabetically by author.

- Bartlett, Tim - **The Book of Navigation** - Copyright 2009, Skyhorse Publishing, 555 Eighth Ave, Suite 903, NYC, NY10018
- Budworth, Geoffrey - **The Complete Book of Knots** - Copyright 1997, The Lyons Press, 123 W 18th St., NYC, NY 10011
- Brotherton, Minor - **The Twelve Volt Bible For Boats** - Copyright 1985, Seven Seas Press/International Marine Publishing, PO Box 220, Camden, ME 04843
- Casey, Don - **Complete Illustrated Sailboat Maintenance Manual** - Copyright 2006 McGraw Hill/International Marine PO Box 220, Camden, ME 04843
- Henderson, Richard - **Essential Seamanship** - Copyright 1994, Cornell Maritime Press, Centerville, MD, 21617
- Rousmaniere, John, - **The Annapolis Book of Seamanship** - Copyright, 1983, 1989, 1999 Simon & Schuster, Rockefeller Center, 1230 Ave of the Americas, NYC, NY 10020

Magazines

- Yachting Magazine
  www.YachtingMagazine.com
- Boating Magazine*
  www.BoatingMag.com
- Power Boat
  www.PowerAndMotorYacht.com
- Wooden Boat
  www.WoodenBoat.com
- Sailing
  SailingMagazine.net
- Good Old Boat
  www.GoodOldBoat.com

online only.

General Reference

- BUC Valu Guide: www.BUC.com
  Used boat value evaluations by year/model
- Defender Marine: www.Defender.com
  Marine supplier
- NAMS: www.NAMSglobal.org
  National Association of Marine Surveyors
- SAMS: www.MarineSurvey.org
  Society of Accredited Marine Surveyors, Inc.
- U.S. Coast Guard National Maritime Center:
  www.DCO.USCG.mil
- United States Power Squadrons®: www.USPS.org
  A nonprofit membership organization that promotes safe boating through education, civic activities and fellowship.
- West Marine: www.WestMarine.com
  Marine supplier

- YachtWorld: www.YachtWorld.com
  Boats for sale

Yacht Brokers Organizations

- California Yacht Brokers Association (CYBA)
  www.CYBA.info
- Certified Professional Yacht Brokers (CPYB)
  www.CPYB.net
- International Yacht Brokers Association, Inc. (IYBA)
  www.InternationalYachtBrokersAssociation.com
- Northwest Yacht Brokers Association (NWYBA)
  www.NwYachtBrokers.com
- Association of Yacht Sales Professionals (YBAA)
  www.YBAA.org

Glossary

Below is a partial list of nautical terms I have compiled to help you "navigate" the sales process for your first boat while (hopefully) avoiding sounding like a complete *"landlubber"* (see landlubber). For a complete list, go to **The Annapolis Book of Seamanship** (see Reference Books) and of course, the World Wide Web.

A

Abaft - Behind, toward the back of the vessel(stern) i.e. "Abaft the mast."

Abeam - At right angles to the boat.

Aboard - On a boat.

Aground - Stuck on the (water's) bottom.

Aloft - In the rigging above the deck.

Alongside - Beside.

Amidship(s) - In the middle of the boat.

Astern - Behind the boat.

Athwartships - Across the boat.

Auxiliary - A sailboat that has an engine.

B

Backstay - A stay running aft from the upper part of the mast.

Beam - A boat's greatest width.

Below - Beneath the deck.

Bend on sails - To install sails on the boom and the headstay.

Berth - (1) A boat's position when tied to a pier or float. (2) A wide berth is a large margin of safety. (3) A bed on a boat.

Bilge - The lowest part of a boat's hull.

Block - A pulley on a boat.

Boat speed - Speed through the water.

Bow - The most forward part of the boat.

Broach (ing) - To veer or yaw dangerously so as to lie broadside to the waves.

Broadside - With the side of the vessel forward or toward a given point: sideways to the waves.

Bulkhead - A wall below the deck that provides athwartship support for the hull.

Buoy - A floating object marking a channel, an obstruction, or a mooring.

Buoyancy - The upward force that keeps the boat floating.

C

Cabin - A room in a boat.

Cast off - To let go a line.

Chain plate - A strap on the hull of a sailboat to which stays are connected.

Chine - The intersection between the topsides and the boat's bottom. A hard chine makes a sharp turn.

Chock - A fairlead for the anchor rode and docking lines.

Chop - Short, steep waves.

Cleat - A wooden, plastic, or metal object to which lines under strain are secured.

Clevis - U-shaped piece that has holes at the end of the prongs to accept the Clevis pin.

Clevis pin - Similar to a bolt but only partially threaded or unthreaded with a cross-hole for a split pin.

COLREGS - The Convention on the International Regulations for Preventing Collisions at Sea (1972).

Coil - To arrange a line or rope in easily manageable loops so it can be stowed.

Companionway - Steps leading down from the deck to the cabin.

Cotter pin - A small pin used to secure a clevis pin and to keep turnbuckles from unwinding.

D

Daysailer - A boat without a cabin that is used for short sails or racing.

Dead - Exactly, such as "dead ahead" or "dead astern"

Deadrise - Measurement based on a combination of linear inches or centimeters and expressed as an angle. The greater the "V" of the hull, the greater the deadrise of the power boat.

Dinghy - A small light boat.

Displacement - A boat's weight — more accurately, the weight of the water the boat displaces.

Dodger - A fold-up spray shield at the forward end of the cockpit. On some boats the shield may be fixed and constructed from fiberglass.

Double Bottom - A watertight compartment between the bottom and the sole, or floor.

Douse - To lower as in "douse the headsail."

Draft (Draught) - The boat's depth below the waterline.

Drag - (1) Resistance. (2) When an anchor breaks out and skips along the bottom.

Drift - A current's velocity; how it affects the forward direction (over the ground) of a vessel under power or sail.

E

Ease - On a sailboat; To let out a sheet in order to fill the sail or to reduce pull on the helm. On a power boat: done by altering course to reduce rolling or broaching.

Ebb - The dropping, outgoing tide.

Eddy - A circular current.

GLOSSARY

F

Fairlead - A fitting through which a line passes to avoid chafing.

Fairway - The middle of a channel, usually marked with buoys ("cans" and/or "nuns").

Fake - To make large loops on deck with a line in order to eliminate kinks.

Fastening - A screw or bolt.

Fender - A rubber bumper hung between the boat and a float, a pier or another boat to protect the boat's topsides.

Fitting - A small often standardized part or piece of gear.

Flood - The rising incoming tide.

Following sea - Waves from astern.

Fore and aft - Everywhere on the boat.

Freeboard - The distance from the deck to the water, or the height of the topsides.

Furl - to roll up and secure a sail to a boom or a stay.

G

Galley - A boat's kitchen.

Gangway - An opening in the lifelines to facilitate boarding from a float or another boat.

Gear - Equipment.

Gimbals - Supports that allow a compass or stove to remain level as the boat heels or is moved about in the waves.

Give-way vessel - The vessel that does not have the right of way.

Ground Tackle - The anchor and anchor rode.

Gunwale (pronounced "gun'l") - A boat's rail at the edge of the deck.

Gust - A strong puff of wind.

H

Halyard - A line or wire rope that hoists a sail and keeps it up.

Hatch - An opening in the deck covered by a hatch cover.

Haul in - (1) Trim a sail. (2) Pull on board such as the dinghy's painter.

Heading - The course one steers.

Headway - Forward motion of a vessel through the water.

Heave - Throw, as in a line.

Heave-to - A process of stopping a sailboat's forward motion by back winding the headsail and easing the mainsail, thereby keeping the boat headed just off the headwind.

Heavy Weather - Rough seas and strong winds.

Heel - A (sail) boat's athwartships tilt.

Helm - (1) A sailboat's tiller or steering station. (2) The sailboat's tendency to head off course: with weather helm, the vessel tends to head up, with lee helm, to head off (down).

Hull - A boat's shell, exclusive of appendages, deck, cabin, and rig.

Hull Speed - The maximum speed of any displacement hull. – governed by the simple formula: $HS = 1.34 \times \sqrt{} \text{ of LWL}$.

I

Inboard - In from the rail.

Inflatable - (1) A life jacket, life raft, or other safety device that must be inflated. (2) A rubber dinghy that needs to be inflated.

J

Jackline - A line, wire, or strap on deck onto which safety harness tethers are clipped.

GLOSSARY

Jackstay - A short stay running from the foredeck to the mast; also babystay.

Jib - A sail carried on the headstay or forestay; aka, headsail, foresail.

Jibe - To change tacks by heading off (the wind) until the sails swing across the boat.

K

Keel - An appendage or fin on the boat's bottom that provides deep ballast and lateral area.

Ketch - A two-masted boat. The aft mast, aka the mizzenmast, is shorter than the mainmast, and is stepped (put in place) forward of the rudder.

L

Landlubber - A person unfamiliar with being on the sea.

Lanyard - A short line.

Lash - To tie.

Lead - (pronounced "*leed*") 1. *N* - A block for a sheet. (2) *V*- to pass a line through a block or fairlead.

Lee, Leeward - Downwind.

Leeway - Side-slippage to leeward

Line - Any length of rope that has a particular use on a boat.

Lubber's line - A post in a compass used to determine the course or a bearing.

M

Magnetic - Relative to magnetic north versus true north.

Make fast - To cleat a line.

Mast step - The support for the bottom (heel or butt) of the mainmast.

Motor sailor - A sailboat with an especially large engine; often considered a hybrid motor boat/sailboat.

N

Nautical mile - 1.15 statute miles. 1 knot = 1 nautical mile per hour.

Navigational Rules - The United States inland and the international (COLREGS) rules for preventing collisions: Aka "rules of the road."

O

Offshore - (1) Out of site of land. (2) Wind direction from the land toward the water.

On board - On a boat.

Onshore - Wind direction from the water toward the land.

One-Design - A single design to which many sister ships are built.

Open boat - A boat without a deck.

Outboard - (1) Out toward and beyond the rail. (2) A retractable engine mounted on the stern.

Overhang - The distance the bow and stern extend beyond the waterline.

P

Padeye - A metal loop to which blocks and shackles are secured.

Painter - A bow line on a dinghy.

Pay out - To ease as in a line or anchor rode.

PFD - Personal Flotation device — the official term for a life jacket.

Pier - A platform on posts that sticks out from the shore.

Plane(ing) - A type of hull that at high speed, rises out of the water.

Pocket Listing - Broker's term for a vessel that is not officially for sale on the open market, but is available.

Port - (1) The left side of the vessel when facing forward. (2) A small window. (3) A commercial harbor.

Porthole - A small round window; aka "port."

Pulpit - A stainless-steel guardrail around the bow or stern

GLOSSARY

R

Race - (1) An especially strong current within a geographical area. (2) An organized competition.

Rhumb line - The most direct course between two points.

Right of way - The legal authority to stay on the present course under the Navigation Rules.

Rode - The anchor line (rope not chain).

Running lights - Lights on a boat illuminated under way at night.

S

Scupper - A deck or cockpit drain.

Seacock - A valve opening and closing a pipe through the hull.

Sea kindly - Comfortable in rough seas.

Sea Room - Enough room from shore and shoals for safe maneuvering.

Seaway - Rough seawater.

Seaworthy - Able to survive heavy weather.

Secure - To fasten or cleat.

Sheer - The curve of the rail.

Skeg - A small fixed fin attached to the underbody near the stern.

Sole - A cabin or cockpit floor.

Speed made good - A boat's speed relative to land; also velocity made good (VMG).

Stand-on vessel - The boat with right-of-way.

Starboard - The right side of the vessel facing forward.

Stay - A large strong rope, usually of wire used to support a mast.

Stow - To put in its proper place on board.

T

Tackle ("block and tackle") - A system of line and blocks that increases hauling power.

Topsides - The outer sides of the hull (not to be confused with the "deck").

Transom - The athwartships-running surface at the stern.

Trim - (1) To adjust a sail to a desired position. (2) To cause (as a boat/dinghy) to assume a desirable position in the water by arrangement of ballast.

Two-Block - To raise all the way.

U

Underbody - The part of the hull that is underwater.

Under power - With the engine on.

Under way - Moving.

Upwind - Toward the direction from which the wind blows.

USCG - United States Coast Guard.

V

Variation - The local difference in degrees between true and magnetic directions.

Veer - A clockwise shift in the wind direction.

W

Waterline - The boat at the water's surface.

Weather Helm - A sailboat's tendency to head up into the wind.

Weigh anchor - Raise the anchor.

Winch - A geared drum used to pull lines.

Windage - Wind resistance.

Y

Yacht - A well-built pleasure boat of a larger size.

Yaw - A side to side movement of a vessel, usually caused by waves.

About the Author

Craig Pierce spent his first eighteen summers in Blue Hill, Maine. He got his first boat, an 8' sailing dinghy called a Turnabout (which everyone who's ever sailed

one knows should be renamed a Turn OVER) at the age of seven. In the following years, he graduated to Mercury class sailboats (15') and "Bullseyes" (16') both built by Cape Cod Yachts. His family had several power boats during that time as well, the last a 32' Robert Rich designed Classic wooden "Downeast" style cruiser which the family took cruising throughout Blue Hill and Penobscot Bays. In the early sixties, his father purchased a Hinckley Sou'wester jr. (30') and Craig, being the only sailor in the family (his father was a "Stink potter" and his mother got seasick), got to "captain" the boat on day trips as well as cruises up and down the Maine Coast.

The owner of three sailboats, Craig has cruised the East and West Coast of the U.S. as well as Nova Scotia, the Bahamas and the Virgin Islands. A professional Yacht Broker in California for ten years, he presently lives in Boston with his life partner, surrounded by their children and grandchildren. Recently he sold his latest — hopefully not his last — boat and is happily searching the virtual boatyards on the Internet for the next one.

Contact Craig at fcpiercewriter@gmail.com. Website: www.fcpierce.com

Notes

Notes

Notes

Notes

Notes

Notes

Notes

Notes

Notes

Notes

BUYING YOUR FIRST BOAT

www.ingramcontent.com/pod-product-compliance
Lightning Source LLC
Chambersburg PA
CBHW071306040426
42444CB00009B/1886